SHARED SPACES

poems by

Roger Jones

Finishing Line Press
Georgetown, Kentucky

SHARED SPACES

Copyright © 2023 by Roger Jones
ISBN 979-8-88838-408-4 First Edition
All rights reserved under International and Pan-American Copyright Conventions. No part of this book may be reproduced in any manner whatsoever without written permission from the publisher, except in the case of brief quotations embodied in critical articles and reviews.

ACKNOWLEDGMENTS

Grateful appreciations to the following journals in which the poems in the collection first appeared:

Concho River Review; Contemporary Haibun Online; Cortland Review; Haibun Today; Louisiana Literature; Poem; RE:Artes Liberales; Red River Review; Ribbons; Salt Creek Review; Small Pond; Southern Poetry Review; Texas Review; TinyWords; Town Creek Poetry Journal; 2Rivers

"The Bee Tree" and "Bait" also appeared in *Southern Poetry Review VIII: Texas* edited by William Wright and Paul Ruffin; published by Texas Review Press.

"My Grandmother Visits" was published in *Strata*, Texas Review Press, Huntsville, TX, 1993.

Publisher: Leah Huete de Maines
Editor: Christen Kincaid
Cover Art: Rene LeBlanc
Author Photo: Roger Jones
Cover Design: Elizabeth Maines McCleavy

Order online: www.finishinglinepress.com
also available on amazon.com

Author inquiries and mail orders:
Finishing Line Press
PO Box 1626
Georgetown, Kentucky 40324
USA

Table of Contents

The Bee Tree 1

Somewhere in Arkansas 2

Plowing 3

Milk 4

Dry Hole 5

Compost 6

My Grandmother Visits 7

Pea-Picking 8

The Louisiana Story (1949) 9

Bait 10

Fishing on Lake Rayburn 12

Shared Spaces 13

Old Fashioned Telephone 14

Hay Hauling 15

Part of a Folk Tale 16

Government Bridge 17

Hunters Returning 19

Butterfly Ranching 20

Mid-August News 21

Fallow 22

Paul Ruffin, friend and mentor

THE BEE TREE

I would like to have found the bee tree,
rumored by the previous owner
to exist somewhere on this land.
Never quite sure where it was,
he never found it himself. Nor
provided us a map, verbal or literal,
though he was sure it was there,
somewhere. Years I crashed through
tons of leaves in woods, searching
out-of-the-way places. No sign.
I was certain it would signal me
by sound, singular humming,
thousands of bees in one place,
at work, holed up in some massive log
or hickory trunk, the front split open
like a mansion door, the wood
charred by lightning or fire.

In my mind the tree still rises like legend;
its energy fills the backwoods like
unverified gossip. What I've found
are mute acres, trees, pathless
routes, groves, small growth rising
from the cedary floor in pure un-
eventfulness, while the legend hums
elsewhere, elusive, a product of pure
hearsay passed down to us over years,
owner to owner, filling our minds
with buzzing curiosity, our brains
like hives overworked with things
we want, but cannot be certain are so.

SOMEWHERE IN ARKANSAS

Long after they moved, the house was burned down for insurance. The rain cistern was emptied, its metal hauled off for scrap. The weeping willow was dozed off and sawed up. The fences were taken down. Who knows what happened to the barn?—an empty space now. Some subsequent owner moved a small trashy frame house onto the lot. It sits unoccupied, windows broken, front door swung wide open. The small beech and silver-leafed trees in the back yard still stand. The grasses are tall, the weeds high. No sign of the garden plot, or the fences that marked its boundaries. They always sensed, and talked about, a wildness they felt in the land. Now that wildness, they conclude, has returned to reclaim it.

sober in the kitchen,
drunk when he reaches the front door
muscadine wine

PLOWING

> *the nothing that is not there,*
> *and the nothing that is.*
> —Wallace Stevens

You'll think at first there's nothing in the center.
You'll trawl around, around, dragging the plow,
turning and sluffing heavy slabs of earth,
loaves and piles folding and unfurling
behind you, dark, damp, root-riddled.
You'll circle all day around nothing but space,
deep grass, and a zero on the fringes.

Meanwhile the sun bears down like a heavy hand;
the wind wafts swales of early clouds across;
the center's out there, and you move inexorably
towards it, but by day's end when you turn
up the full pasture and look back over your shoulder
at what's complete, you see: before, the center
was nowhere particular. Now it's the whole field.

MILK

Early spring, the rainy season.
The road's a greasy red slop,
already cut by six a.m. by neighbors' trucks—
ruts so deep my mother and I stumble
as we walk the muddy bend around to
Hannah Lee's farmhouse, glass gallon
milk jars weighty in our hands.
In the kitchen, Hannah spills milk
straight from the pail into our jars,
each scummed with an oily butter rainbow
and tasting of field grass, the hint of thistle.
Later, walking home, I hear the milk
slosh and gloop against the lid.
The cold wind tags our faces
the green-tipped roadside woods,
the bare blackberry vines toppling over fences.
Each puddle in the road's a muddy pool.
A few blowzy primroses stir and waggle
in the raw gray morning air.

DRY HOLE

Originally, just old-growth forest.
The owner said to live in another state.
We liked it for its loblollies, white pines, sweet gum;
for the high hard hickories and canopy ash,
the thick undergrowth of brambles and blackberries
tumbling in spring over rusting fences,
with now and then a rabbit bounding through.

That year wildcatters with their maps
knew every working well in the county,
every hole that had been abandoned, how far down
each had gone. They had seismic maps of sub-
strata, wavy lines outlining each ripple
and contour under the earth we walked on.
With big machines, they came and cut an easement

to where they wanted to drill. Huge wheels
left sticky red clay tracks looping on and off.
They piled up heaps of pine slash to rust and burn
in fall, trucked the logs off to mill, and settled in
for the haul. Through trees we could hear loud
gargling motors, at night see lights high
atop the rig. All those who lived close hoped

he or she would be part of the collective pool.
We scrutinized each coming and going
for signs. Nothing came of it, and come late
winter, when leaves had fallen, and stars were bright,
the company folded its rig, absorbed the loss
and moved on; we were left with an open muddy field,
a wide clay scab on the landscape, like a trauma

we could never shed, no matter how deep the grass
of coming spring, or how bright the flowers.

COMPOST

earthworms
stitching through rubble
knit rich seething
hulks of leaves,
sawdust, rank decay
:
a silent heat
breaks down the bottom
like coffee grounds,
where the round wire bin
stores weeks
:
trees and plants coalesce—
a meshed pile
loosely fallen, time
lying quiet
below a net of clouds
:
all seasons descend
on our supply, so many
years—a stash we turn
& sift to find, again,
our lives

MY GRANDMOTHER'S VISITS

Always from her suitcase, a sigh of diesel
from bus stations, the breezy gust of arrivals
and departures. She'd settle into her room,
then direct us down some stray, neglected highway—
hillsides, pastures, cows, hedgerows, hayfields.
Buckling exhausted houses. Acres of cottonfields

no different than when she'd gone down them
as a child, dragging a heavy sack. Glades fell open.
Each direction wrote its name, and whole histories
dropped out of the patchwork counties. Beside her,
I dreamed back places she'd mentioned,
a scent of tobacco on her old breath. She'd sit

quiet for a moment, then spot some house
and start all over: sumac, dogwood, sassafras. . .
My father wheeled her past the stiles of fences,
taking first this direction then that, while
she breathed the heady acres, and Back Then
trundled behind us like a faithful wagon.

PEA PICKING

A bright dry morning
before the July blast begins
again in the garden. Crouched,

heads wrapped, they move
slowly up the last rows.
Bee-quick fingers leap to snap

pods bobbing under sagging string.
I can see on Papa's work shirt
two blue hoops of sweat

as he waves the others in:
uncles, grandparents, neighbors.
The oaks behind us rise, green

tops screaming with cicadas.
In breathless air the river lets go
its dank breath of rot.

My cousins and I, too young
to pick, are swinging legs
from the pick-up's tailgate;

beside us, the stacks
of upside-down bushel baskets
yet to fill and the baskets

already full on the ground, bulging
with mazes of long purple pods.
Shelled, in a bowl, the peas

will stare up, sightless eyes;
and on Mother's fingers, a stain appear
dark as love, blood, or blood-kin.

THE LOUISIANA STORY (1949)

In Robert Flaherty's film, as young Latour
poles his pirogue through the Atchafalaya,
the clatter and clanging of Standard Oil's big derrick
seems mirthful, indigenous to landscape.
It's post-World War Two. The industry put to use
to vaporize cities and fuel task forces
and invasion armies may now just as easily
slip up the local bayou and set up shop
in the vegetal waters near home. And who
in the story seems worried? Smiles abound.
The rig men are infectiously avuncular;
the boy's main consternation's not with the rig
but with his miscreant raccoon, who prowls along
fulfilling its wildness. The nearest oil slick
one might find's still twenty years away.
By that time, Latour's grown, the petroleum
in the swamp long tapped, the new wells far offshore.
For now the sumptuous bayou's summer light
sparkles infectiously. Work and play relax
side by side. Only a wily gator, rumored
to be somewhere in the swamp, lurks nearby
to menace the garden and its benign machine.

BAIT

Certain hot evenings those summers
my father would pull up to Jewel's red-
and-white checkered butcher shop
on the edge of town, give me a few
wrinkled dollars, and I'd go inside to buy
for us all a fresh new cow heart to use
for fish bait at the pond. I'd step
into refrigerated air, the lobby with its
counters and stools, its trio of old men
loitering in chairs to ramble hours about
typical nothings. I'd give my order
to Jewel, the decorated vet, who stood
apart listening at the register.
Hunkered and odd, he'd grimace;
I'd flinch behind his back at his
fixed eye, his distance, the grayish
pallor of hands and face. He carried
like a secret (so my father had said)
within his body the residual bones of
shrapnel from an old battle, though
no one, not even wife, could coax him
to give up what he knew. On the wall,
he kept a picture of a cow cut up
by dotted lines into shapes like countries
soldiers had been driven across weeks
as the war waned. From the gray cavernous
confines of his lobby, he turned
and disappeared with my order into
the back shop, with its odors
of cow blood and hosed concrete.
Then he'd return, and I'd hand him
my money; he'd nod a grave thank you
and heft across to me the heavy heart
wrapped up like an artifact. In both hands,
I'd take it, sheathed in its stiff

white paper, seams taped, folds
and corners thorn-crisp, and one
edge matted ever so slightly
with the moist ooze of blood.

FISHING ON LAKE RAYBURN

Ghostly morning mist seeps up
this way on the gray water at dawn.
The boat ticks and hums, the swish-
ripple of lake water along the gunnels
as we paddle to tie up on a tree stob
like a finger in the center, gone
last year when floods rising all over
left no landmarks. Sitting on water
this still, watching trees sift out of fog
and dark, I'm reading a slow book
of the world, gathering knowledge.
Somewhere across the water,
a heron sends its rust-hinge cry,
Scrorck!; a woodpecker types
its name in the top of a pine.

Last night's nail-thin crescent
still tilts above the treeline just
over the cove, and on the other shore,
the old retiree who haunts this lake
every morning poles his boat
around the bank, sweeping minnows
into a net. He waves at me as I
send my first cast singing off
and feel the chop-churn of buzz-bait
chew the top water towards me
just before the bass rising
sends up my arms that jolt,
true, hard, and sudden
as June's hook of lightning.

SHARED SPACES

The Wal-Mart mechanic motions me from the lobby door.
I follow him into the garage, to my car.

"Look-a here." He points under the raised hood.

Over a dozen acorns inside the lidless air filter manifold,
side by side in a ring around the metal outer covering.

"How ya figure those got there?"

I shake my head, but I have a hunch: field mice
near home crawling up from the ground into hoses,
through small dark airless openings, into the tightly shut
manifold under my closed hood. Back out again.

Raccoons, possums, armadillos, field rats, deer, scorpions,
foxes, daddy-longlegs, spiders, humans. So many lives here;

anything can happen.

among head-high sunflowers
a murmur of bees
in our ears

OLD FASHIONED TELEPHONE

Voices crackling back along the party line:
"Power's out down here, too"—
old Louie Champion, up at his timbered lot.

A stormy April night.
We're by transistor radios, alone,
eager to see where bad weather's headed—

eight dark houses, up and down
a dirt road that dead ends at Denman's farm.
Mrs. Estes chiming in, "I heard

there was a twister down in Dalby."
Then Mack Roberts: "something in it.
Sure been wild down here."

Back and forth, like a current,
the news in the dark
running its route, while candle-flames at home

leap and waggle in the window pane,
one wide pine outside profiled black
in lightning's backdrop sheet, and bullet rain.

HAY HAULING

We lived for dusky moments, each hayfield
cleared, every bale bound up with wire,
stacked on the flatbed, loaded into the barn
with gaps between each bale for air. We
plucked them all up, even the bad-scented bale
we lifted to find a half-rotten cottonmouth
squeezed between the wires. Rolling out
again to the water cooler down on the fence line—
the hedgerows' shadows of human forms rising
at us, the air filling with the inhuman screech
of insects— we watched the sun flatten, a red
drop poised above the world we knew. Our limbs
and muscles ached to a new star pulsing
Work just over the ochred sky. And southward,
that orange-topped thunderhead we prayed to
all afternoon, that grumbled and gave us hope,
broke up at the end, tore apart, and wisped away.

PART OF A FOLK TALE

Thing is, after the man shot the armadillo,
the dog wouldn't let the poor thing lie.
First the man buried it behind the barn,
out of the dog's sight—so he thought.
Somehow the dog found it, dug it up,
left it in the back yard. So the man
re-buried it, this time farther in a field,
and walked off wiping his hands thinking
That's that. But the dog unearthed it again,
in two pieces and lay one by the oak tree.
By now the odor was rising. The man
whipped the dog, and buried the pieces
far out behind the high corn. He leaned
the shovel against the barn and sighed, *That
will do it.* But that night, as he lay down
in the room's hot summer dark beside
his bride, and reached across the moonless
space, and the death odor outside
seeped through an opened window,
what did he think? Rising, he looked out
to see the dog panting, near the porch,
on which the seething, formless flesh
lay, dropped before the master like a gift,
under the very window of the room
where only moments before the man
and his wife lay so quiet in bed, touching.

GOVERNMENT BRIDGE

Old as our town the iron swing bridge
was a dreadful, cantilevered relic with bars,
pulleys, and a deep fearful air
of the mechanical sublime. It rattled me
as a child, hulking
impersonal across from its bank
on the island like a rustling dinosaur—
far more frightful at night,
when the wide river ran past town
in darkness, a constant *shirr* one couldn't unhear,
making us see it even more vividly inward.

Out of dense night air and eternal pulse
of river, a plaintive horn
would signal, a red light
appear in the distance, and the bridge
would go into its clanking, clattering
motion, a dirge of metallic scrapes
along unseen tracks, lopsided pulleys,
as half the bridge soon stood alone
across the way, and the nearer half
swung broadside to the flow. Soon

the dimly-lit passing craft—barge
most often, or riverboat—would glide
noiselessly through. From a bank
we could see the other side
of a severed highway in darkness,
a few lonely sprinkled lights suspended
there, the road itself
like an abruptly-halted thought,
a sheer drop in space to the unseen abyss

below. We held our breath
in fear of non-endings. But in time the inhuman
creak and iron shudder of the retracted side
would commence again, in reverse;
the intersected commerce
of road to road, to the island itself ,
would resume its duty, while starless night
and river, rejoined, surged on.

HUNTERS, RETURNING

The antlered buck killed,
slung over the Chevy's hood.
The open-eyed head lobbed over
the edge, tongue out, blood
from the mouth scrawled down
the car's side like lightning,
like a signature.

BUTTERFLY RANCHING

Mid-summer and the American snout butterflies are passing through on regular migration. This year, because of drought, the yellow jackets are missing; the snouts have the run of things. In summer's record heat, huge numbers of them hang out in trees, hackberries their favorites. Early afternoons, I step outside, turn on a hose, and adjust the nozzle so I can spread a light coat of water all over the blistering dust and dying lawn grass. As if shaken out of limbs and leaves, butterflies cascade down immediately. I find myself surrounded as they descend, as in a singular cloud, from trees to wet hot-scented earth—fluttering and motion, as if by design.

bright sunlight on the barn wall
I lean a shovel
against its thin shadow

MID-AUGUST NEWS

Here come the gaping days of languid heat
to check off one by one and file aside.
Swelter's not exact enough a word,
but close as we can come. Leaves unbind,
early floaters, premature, before the first
fronts push through a brush of chill.
Once-chunky berry bushes thin back more
austere, their berries tipped red before

final flaring. Soon, we're left with
What Is rapidly becoming *What Was,*
a little weariness, the sense this month was
meant for the land to lean back on what has
already come. Meanwhile, a half-moon slips
away; days start to shorten and go slack.
Now and then a message meanders in: no news
but of others from afar just hanging on likewise

FALLOW

I always wondered who planted them in the neighboring field, a double row of yellow daffodils, up each spring, winding toward nothing, as if arriving at an invisible porch, invisible house.

voices echoing
deep in woods—
lives we might have lived

Roger Jones earned his PhD from Oklahoma State University in 1986, and has taught at Lamar University in Beaumont, TX and Texas State University in San Marcos. He is a member of the Master of Fine Arts poetry program at Texas State. He has published three poetry collections from Texas Review Press: *Remembering New London* (1981), *Strata* (1993), and *Are We There Yet?* (2008). His chapbook *Familial* was published in 2015 by Finishing Line Press. An electronic chapbook of Japanese haibun, *Goodbye*, was awarded the Snapshot Press e-chapbook award in 2012 and was published in 2017.

His poems have appeared since the 1970s in journals such as *Kansas Quarterly, Arkansas Review, Poet Lore, Cortland Review, Southern Poetry Review, California Quarterly, Modern Haiku, Ribbons, Cimarron Review* and *Louisiana Literature,* among others.

www.ingramcontent.com/pod-product-compliance
Lightning Source LLC
Chambersburg PA
CBHW022107080426
42734CB00009B/1507